A S

COPYRIGHT NOTICE

Dear valued reader,

Thank you for purchasing my Book. I have poured my heart and soul into creating this comprehensive guide designed specifically for you. This Book is the result of extensive research, knowledge, and dedication.

Please note that no part of this document may be reproduced or transmitted in any form by any means (electronic, photocopying, recording, or otherwise) without prior written permission from my publisher.

While every effort has been made to ensure the completeness and accuracy of this Book, there may be room for improvement in typography or content. The primary purpose of my book is to educate and inform.

I, along with my publisher, make no representations or warranties with respect to the accuracy or completeness of the contents of this book. We will not be held liable or responsible to any person or entity for any loss or damage caused or alleged to have been caused, directly or indirectly, by the information contained in this book.

Please note that the content provided is for informational purposes only and may not be suitable for your specific situation. If you need professional help, it is recommended that you consult with a qualified therapist or psychiatrist.

Thank you for your understanding and support.

COPYRIGHT © 2023 - 2024

For my princess...

♥

I want to dedicate this book to my proudest accomplishment, my beautiful daughter Selena. Everything I do and all I am after, my Lord and Savior, is you. Thank you for saving my life. I am so proud of you and all that you have and will accomplish.
I love you, snookums!

Mommie

TABLE OF CONTENTS

Introduction

01 HEALING THE INNER BASICS

02 THE EVOLUTION

03 WHAT IS GODLY FEMININE ENERGY?

04 UNDERSTANDING THE CONNECTION

05 YOUR SUPER POWER IS ALREADY IN YOU

06 LEARNING TO TRUST

07 LEARNING TO FORGIVE YOURSELF AND OTHERS

08 TOOLS TO TAP INTO YOUR GODLY FEMININE ENERGY

09 THE WORKBOOK

Acknowledgements

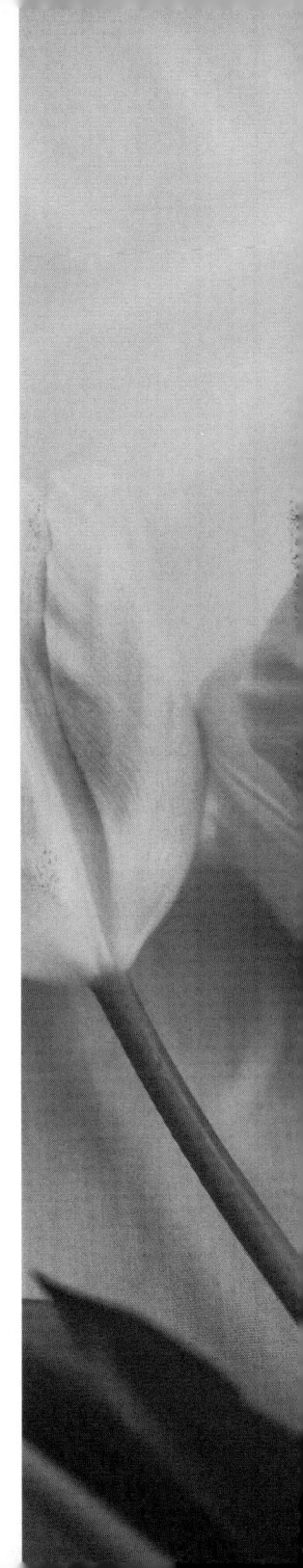

INTRODUCTION

Dear Beautiful One,

Welcome to a transformative journey of self-discovery, empowerment, and healing. This book is an invitation to reconnect with the most profound aspects of your being - your divine feminine energy and your inner child. In a world that often values masculine traits and adult responsibilities, we've sometimes lost touch with our feminine essence and the joyful, innocent little girl within. This book is your guide to reclaiming, celebrating, and integrating these essential parts of yourself.

Within these pages, you'll embark on a dual exploration: embracing your feminine energy in the modern world and rediscovering your inner child, the little girl within. We'll delve into the core principles of feminine power, from nurturing your intuition to embracing your body's innate wisdom. Alongside this, you'll learn to identify, heal, and celebrate your inner child - that playful, creative, and vulnerable part of you that holds the key to your authentic self.

This book will guide you through:
- Connecting deeply with your intuition and inner wisdom
- Embracing and appreciating your feminine body
- Cultivating receptivity and the art of receiving
- Aligning with natural cycles and rhythms
- Expressing your creativity and sensuality
- Practicing self-love and compassion
- Identifying and healing your inner child wounds
- Rediscovering the joy, wonder, and playfulness of your little girl within
- Integrating your healed inner child with your adult self
- Embodying feminine leadership in your personal and professional life

A special focus is placed on the little girl that lives in all of us, her healing and discovery. You'll learn how to recognize signs of her wounding, techniques for communicating with and nurturing your little girl within, and ways to bring more play and wonder into your adult life. As you heal and integrate her, you'll find a new depth to your feminine energy - one that combines the wisdom of your adult self with the spontaneity and joy of your inner little girl.

At the end of this book, you'll find a specially designed workbook. This five-page guide is your personal companion on this journey, offering daily practices and reflections to deepen your connection with your feminine essence and your little girl within.

Remember, embracing your divine feminine and healing your inner little girl is not about perfection. It's a journey of unfolding, of remembering who you truly are at your core. It's about giving yourself permission to be soft and strong, receptive and powerful, intuitive and rational, mature and playful. As you turn these pages, know that you're not just reading a book - you're coming home to your whole, integrated self.

So take a deep breath, open your heart, and let's begin this beautiful journey of embracing your divine feminine and rediscovering your precious little girl within. The Godly feminine woman and the little girl within you are waiting to be awakened and united.

With love, feminine power, and childlike wonder,

Angel

HEALING THE INNER BASICS

01

Healing the inner child
BASICS

WHO IS THAT LITTLE GIRL?

That little girl, the inner child is your friendly, joyful, emotional, and playful feeling side. This aspect of yourself can vary depending on your mood and energy level. At times, you may feel indifferent due to current situations in your outer life. Like the outer child, your inner child is typically happy, blissful, and adventurous. The inner child is also known as the lower third of an extensive model of the human psyche called the "Three Selves."

Psychology experts describe the inner child as the childlike aspect of a person's psyche. It encompasses everything you learned and experienced as a child before puberty. This inner child functions as a semi-independent unit that operates under your conscious mind.

Do you know who she is? The little girl within?
The first task to healing your wounds is getting to know the little girl inside. When you strip away all the painful experiences you have endured, who are you? Who are you before all the societal conditioning, family criticism, or

abusive relationships? Who is that little girl within, in her purest state without all the overthinking, the overanalyzing, or constant worrying? In a world of total safety and freedom, who is she? And trust me, she's in there. We just need to let her know that it's safe to come out. She needs to know that you're here for her and you're going to keep a watchful eye over her. She needs to know you care.

EXPLORING HOW TO HEAL YOUR INNER CHILD

The emotional wounds you have suffered in your childhood may develop with time. Healing your inner child is a process of acknowledging, nurturing, and integrating the wounded parts of your psyche from childhood.

The very first step to take is assessing the wound: Wounds to the feminine spirit usually occur after you suffer the type of experiences that lead to a feeling of shame, blame, regret, or lack of confidence/insecurity. And these negative mental states can lead to suppression of the expression of: Body image & beauty, Love & sex, Emotions & personal expression, Emotions & personal expression. Here are some strategies that I had to do with therapy to heal the little girl inside of me:

STEP 1: EARN THE TRUST YOUR LITTLE GIRL INSIDE

I realized that I had low self-esteem and self-worth as a little girl because I was overweight and had bushy hair. It was hard to trust people's compliments, especially my dimples and naturally curly locks. As an adult, I still had issues with it and began to wound that little girl. She became hidden, so I had to learn to develop trust. To heal her, I needed to regain her confidence; in essence, I needed to trust myself, acknowledge and validate.

This is also one way of treating her. When she is wounded, like a cut or broken bone, she needs treatment. Make sure that your inner child feels accepted and recognizes her true self. You have to help her drive away the guilt and shame. The guilt is something I still sometimes struggle with.

Recognize that your inner child exists and that her feelings are valid. Your little girl inside should understand that you are there to protect and nurture her. In acknowledging her, I had to understand and accept that part of me still carries childhood experiences and emotions, good and bad. Then, I validated those feelings by telling myself it's okay to feel them, even if they seem irrational in my adult life. Those feelings are and were real.

STEP 2: PRACTICE SELF-COMPASSION

You have to help your little girl fight and move on. Be kind and understanding towards yourself, especially when dealing with emotional issues. Try to understand the grief of the little girl inside and learn to embrace her. Forgive her when she didn't fight and move on. Treat yourself with the same kindness you'd offer a close friend. When you make mistakes or face difficulties, respond with understanding rather than harsh self-criticism. I had to learn to "get out of my head," which helped me develop self-compassion. After embracing the pains of your inner child, you are one step ahead for great healing.

Self-compassion involves treating yourself with kindness and understanding, especially during difficult times. It means acknowledging your humanity and imperfections without harsh self-judgment. For women, this can involve:
- Accepting your body and appearance without criticism
- Forgiving yourself for mistakes or perceived shortcomings
- Speaking to yourself with gentleness and care

Self-compassion nurtures the receptive, nurturing aspects of feminine energy. It allows women to embrace their softness and vulnerability, which are traditionally associated with feminine traits. This practice can help balance the often harsh, self-critical voice many women internalize from societal pressures.

STEP 3: PROCESS TRAUMA

Work with a therapist to address any childhood trauma or negative experiences. I thank God every day for the therapist that I have had and the one I am seeing now. One of the hardest things for me to do was confront some of the childhood and adolescence traumas I had. So many of my memories were suppressed. Once I gained her trust, those memories resurfaced, but this time, I had help.

Trauma processing involves acknowledging, understanding, and working through past traumatic experiences. This often requires professional help and may include:
- Identifying traumatic events and their impact on your life
- Learning coping mechanisms for trauma-related symptoms
- Reprocessing traumatic memories to reduce their emotional charge

Processing trauma can help women reclaim parts of themselves that may have been suppressed or damaged. It can restore a sense of safety and trust, allowing for a fuller expression of feminine energy, which often involves openness and connection.

STEP 4: REPARENTING YOURSELF

Provide yourself with the love, support, and guidance you may have needed as a child. Identify the parenting you needed but didn't receive, then consciously provide that for yourself. This might involve setting consistent routines, celebrating your achievements, or comforting yourself during difficult times. It can also mean establishing true boundaries.

Reparenting involves giving yourself the care, guidance, and support you needed but may not have received in childhood. This can include:
- Setting healthy boundaries and routines
- Celebrating your achievements and efforts
- Providing yourself with comfort and reassurance during difficult times

Reparenting can help women cultivate a strong, nurturing inner voice. This aligns with the maternal aspect of feminine energy, allowing women to feel more grounded and secure in expressing their femininity.

STEP 5: PRACTICE FORGIVENESS

Forgiveness involves letting go of resentment and negative feelings towards yourself or others who have hurt you. It doesn't mean forgetting or excusing harmful behavior but freeing yourself from its ongoing impact. This can involve:
- Acknowledging the hurt and its impact on you
- Choosing to release the grudge or negative feelings
- Finding ways to move forward, with or without the person who caused harm

Full transparency, this is tough. I harbored much bitterness after my second failed marriage. I began to suppress that little girl with anger. Then I realized that I needed to forgive her to free her. She is the joy and peace.

Forgiveness is often associated with compassion and emotional intelligence, which are frequently linked to feminine energy. By practicing forgiveness, women can embody feminine energy's transformative and healing aspects, promoting harmony and emotional balance.

STEP 6: EXPRESS EMOTIONS

Emotional expression involves allowing yourself to feel and communicate your emotions authentically. This might include:
- Identifying and naming your feelings
- Finding healthy outlets for emotional expression (art, music, dance, reading, etc.)
- Communicating your emotions clearly to others

In many cultures, feminine energy is associated with emotional depth and expressiveness. By embracing and expressing emotions, women can tap into this aspect of feminine energy, fostering deeper connections with themselves and others.

With these simple tips on how to heal your inner child, you have a chance to embrace a new and exciting life. So, don't underestimate the power of your inner child. Are you ready to heal your inner child? Then, start treating it and you will experience its positive effects in your life.

By engaging in these practices, women can deepen their connection to their feminine energy, leading to greater self-awareness, emotional well-being, and authenticity in their personal expression.

TIPS ON HOW TO DISCOVER YOUR LITTLE GIRL WITHIN

After she is healed and whole, you can now discover your little girl within! She represents joy and peace. When you have peace, you experience a happy and balanced life. Below is roadmap on how to maintain her and you new discovery!

STOP RESTRICTING YOUR ACTIONS

Always consider how impulsive you are now compared to your childhood. Instead of ignoring, listen to the voice that tells you to try something new. I also cultivated receptivity. I began to practice receiving compliments, help, and gifts graciously.
- Allow yourself to act spontaneously and freely
- Release self-imposed limitations and societal expectations
- Embrace your authentic desires and impulses
- Open yourself to new experiences and perspectives

This helps you move from rigid, controlled behavior (often associated with masculine energy) to a more fluid, intuitive way of being. In my second marriage, I had a dominance that fostered insecurity in my ex-husband. I manipulated that energy. I remember telling him he could not discipline my daughter because he was not her biological father. This is something that should have been discussed before the marriage instead of me communicating that I didn't trust his parenting style.

In hindsight, it was a good decision on my part; however, I handled it horribly. Controlling my behavior now encourages receptivity and openness, core aspects of feminine energy.

USE YOUR IMAGINATION

Always allow yourself to be imaginative, both in your actions and thinking. You also need to find creative activities that can kindle your imaginations.

- Engage in creative activities like coloring, storytelling on social media (I love podcasting and blogging), or allowing yourself to daydream!!
- Visualize positive scenarios and outcomes
- Allow your mind to wander and explore new possibilities

Imagination taps into the creative, intuitive side of feminine energy. It encourages you to trust your inner wisdom and embrace the unknown, moving away from the logical, action-oriented masculine energy.

TAKE TIME TO LAUGH AND SMILE

Everyone has a problem in life. But it doesn't mean that you have a reason not to smile. Even just saying the word smile, makes you smile! When I was at my lowest post-divorce, pre-healing journey, I used to listen to Kirk Franklin's song "Smile." I would cry and cry, then smile. Eventually, I smiled the entire song.

Find some activities to make your life more interesting and exciting. Engage in activities that bring you joy. Remember that little girl is joy! Depending on your choice:
- you can play with children or grandchildren,
- listen to your favorite music, or watch hilarious movies.
- Seek out humor in daily life
- Surround yourself with positive, uplifting people

Laughter and joy are expressive and emotional, aligning with feminine energy. This helps shift from the serious, goal-oriented masculine energy to a more light-hearted, present-moment feminine energy.

ENGAGE YOUR WORLD USING YOUR SENSES

Simply reflect on how the world seemed brighter when you were young.
- Practice mindfulness by focusing on what you can see, hear, smell, taste, and touch
- Enjoy sensory experiences like aromatherapy, massage, or praying/meditation
- Pay attention to the textures, colors, and sensations around you
- Spend time outdoors, observing natural beauty
- Care for plants or animals
- Recognize your connection to the natural world

Sensory engagement connects you with your body and the present moment, core aspects of feminine energy. This shifts focus from the doing and achieving of masculine energy to the being and experiencing of feminine energy.

"AFTER SHE IS HEALED AND WHOLE, YOU CAN NOW DISCOVER YOUR LITTLE GIRL WITHIN! SHE REPRESENTS JOY AND PEACE. WHEN YOU HAVE PEACE, YOU EXPERIENCE A HAPPY AND BALANCED LIFE."

With these simple steps, you can start discovering your healed little girl. Remember, balance is key. The goal isn't to completely eliminate masculine energy but to cultivate a harmonious blend that allows your feminine energy to flourish. This process of discovery and nurturing your inner little girl can lead to a more joyful, peaceful, and balanced life!

THE EVOLUTION

02

"*To* take away bad memories and pains in the past, you need to understand the healing of your inner child. Through this inner child self work, you can heal your mind and soul. You also have a chance to recover the self-confidence to forgive and forget the pain. As a result, you will live in a better and happy life., your true Godly Femininity!"

The evolved woman who has embraced her feminine energy and healed her inner child typically embodies several key qualities and behaviors. Here's a picture of what this evolved, feminine woman might look like.

She is self-assured and confident, emotionally intelligent, intuitive and trusting. When a women has evolved and healed the wound girl inside, she becomes more nurturing, most compasionate. One of the things, I noticed in me, is that I became sensually aware. It is easy for me to be in touch with my body and what it needs. I am no longer ashamed of the changes menuopause hands to me.

Women in this period of evolution moves with grace and fluidity. We began to evolve with welcoming new experiences and become more open. Then God in His infinite wisdom, shows us how to embody love and compassion, versus bitterness and lust.

The evolved feminine woman exudes a quiet confidence that comes from deep self-assurance. She's comfortable in her own skin, embracing her unique qualities without the need for comparison. This self-love radiates outward, creating a magnetic presence. Her emotional intelligence is highly developed; she's attuned to her own feelings and those of others, expressing herself with authenticity and grace. This woman trusts her intuition implicitly, making decisions that honor both her logical mind and her inner wisdom. She navigates life's uncertainties with a sense of flow, trusting in the journey.

Nurturing and compassionate, she creates supportive environments for herself and others, always maintaining healthy boundaries. Her sensual awareness is heightened; she's deeply connected to her body and its needs, moving through life with fluidity and grace. This woman is open and receptive, welcoming new experiences and perspectives with enthusiasm. She's comfortable receiving as well as giving, understanding that this receptivity is a strength, not a weakness. Spiritually, she feels a profound connection to something greater than herself, embodying love and compassion in her daily interactions. She finds meaning in life's experiences, big and small, and practices gratitude as a way of being. This spiritual connection infuses her life with purpose and deepens her impact on the world around her.

This evolved, feminine woman has not eliminated her masculine traits but has found a harmonious balance. She can be assertive when needed, but leads primarily with her feminine strengths. She's not perfect, but she embraces her imperfections as part of her unique journey.

The journey to this evolved state is ongoing. It involves continuous self-reflection, growth, and a commitment to living authentically. As she evolves, a woman may find that she naturally inspires and uplifts those around her, creating a ripple effect of positive feminine energy in her community and beyond.

Remember, there's no one "right" way to be feminine. Each woman's expression of feminine energy will be unique to her, influenced by her personality, culture, and life experiences. The key is to embrace and nurture your authentic self, allowing your inner feminine energy to shine through in a way that feels true to you.

WHAT IS FEMININE ENERGY?

03

What is Feminine Energy?

*F*eminine energy is a concept that refers to a set of qualities, traits, and principles traditionally associated with the feminine aspect of human nature. It's important to note that feminine energy is not exclusive to women; all individuals, regardless of gender, possess both feminine and masculine energies to varying degrees.

characteristcs of heightened feminine
energy specifically in women...

Receptivity and openness:
- Being open to receiving ideas, help, and experiences
- Willingness to listen and absorb information

Intuition and inner wisdom:
- Trusting gut feelings and inner knowing
- Making decisions based on instinct as well as logic

Nurturing and compassion:
- Caring for others and oneself
- Empathy and emotional support

Creativity and expression:
- Artistic and imaginative pursuits
- Ability to bring ideas into form

Collaboration and community:
- Valuing relationships and connections
- Working together rather than competing

Fluidity and adaptability:
- Going with the flow of life
- Adapting to changing circumstances with grace

Sensuality and embodiment:
- Being in tune with one's body and senses
- Enjoying physical and sensory experiences

Emotional intelligence:
- Understanding and managing emotions effectively
- Expressing feelings authentically

Presence and being:
- Focusing on the present moment
- Valuing states of being over constantly doing

Feminine energy is often described as yin energy in Eastern philosophies, associated with qualities like softness, receptivity, and inward focus. It complements masculine (yang) energy, which is more about action, assertiveness, and outward focus.

Embracing feminine energy doesn't mean rejecting masculine qualities. Instead, it's about finding a balance and allowing these softer, more receptive qualities to flourish alongside the more action-oriented masculine traits. In today's world, cultivating feminine energy can help create more balance, both personally and collectively, leading to a more harmonious and holistic approach to life.

What is the difference between Masculine and Feminine?

Basically, in every individual, there are two energies they carry inside; masculine and feminine energy. Both energies are not determined by gender, and generally one is more dominant than the other. However, with both energies, women predominantly default to feminine, whereas men predominantly default to masculine. So, what do masculine and feminine energy mean? And how do they affect a relationship?

Masculine Energy
As reported by Living Well Counseling Services, masculine energy is about doing and being action-oriented. Masculine energy is stable and more predictable. The strengths are will, clarity, and focus. The masculine energy likes to create structures and rules, so it knows how to apply logic properly.

Masculine energy has core energy or characteristics as follows:
- Good rational and logical skills
- Able to think clearly
- Able to build ongoing effort
- Good external strength in persona
- Able to think creatively and solve problems
- Fond of challenges
- Longing for admiration and appreciation
- Independent

Feminine Energy

Contrary to masculine energy, feminine energy is flowing and dynamic. Its movements cannot be predicted or always explained with a rational mind. This energy is not constrained by social norms because it does not follow any rules other than the guidance that comes from the heart. People who are more dominant with feminine energy will have the following characteristics:

- Easily able to calm down
- Good at taking care of themselves and loving themselves
- Able to find creative inspiration
- Able to empathize
- Able to make judgments outside the realm of rationality
- Prioritizing feelings
- Having good communication skills

How Do These Energies Affect Relationships?

According to Psychology Today, some researchers argue that men's and women's brains are wired differently. The male brain is wired from front to back, with few connections across the two hemispheres. Women, on the other hand, have more wiring from left to right, so the two hemispheres are more interconnected.

Even though everyone can combine both energies without determining gender, masculine and feminine energies are two different polarities. However, each individual has one kind of energy that is way more prominent than the other one. Therefore, these differences can attract another human being to fit the puzzle that one is lacking.

The relationship built by two people can fall into discord when the masculine partner has defaulted too far over their feminine tendencies with their feminine partner, who is also in their feminine tendencies or vice versa. When the polarity is out of balance, the relationship starts to be disharmonic, with more frequent misunderstandings, disconnection, conflict, and, ultimately, a complete break in sexual intimacy.

To solve this conflict caused by imbalanced energy, we don't have to ask our significant other to be more feminine or masculine as we can't control people and their energy, which is not supposed to be something we aim for. However, what we can do to recover from the energy imbalance is by intimate communication where we address the problem and find the solution together.

UNDERSTANDING THE CONNECTION

04

You might wonder why being conscious of your inner child is essential. The answer is simple yet profound. Your inner child represents the aspect of your awareness that is naturally innocent, uncomplicated, and playful. It's the part of you that has a pure, simple connection to spirit and embodies the essence of feminine energy.

If you experienced dysfunction in your childhood, reconnecting with your inner child becomes crucial. This reconnection helps heal past wounds and restore your consciousness to its natural, vibrant state, allowing your feminine energy to flow freely.

To achieve this, start by addressing your basic physical and emotional needs. This might involve nourishing yourself properly, learning to care for others without losing yourself, and cultivating positive emotions. As you heal your inner child, you'll notice an increase in your feminine energy, characterized by heightened intuition, increased emotional intelligence, and a greater capacity for nurturing yourself and others.

Remember, a healed inner child is the foundation for embracing your full feminine power. It allows you to approach life with openness, creativity, and compassion - all hallmarks of high feminine energy. By nurturing your inner child, you're not just healing past wounds; you're unlocking the full potential of your feminine essence.

As you heal your inner child, you open the door to greater spiritual and emotional freedom. This deepened spiritual connection ripples through all areas of your life, enhancing your feminine energy. You'll find yourself more at peace, experiencing greater joy and vitality. Your perspective will shift, allowing you to see the world through a more intuitive, compassionate lens - key aspects of feminine energy.

The concept that everything stems from a single source - the Great Universal Spirit - aligns beautifully with feminine energy principles. This unified view suggests that all elements work in harmony to manifest the Divine Plan. As you develop your spirituality, you become more attuned to these connections, embodying the receptive and interconnected nature of feminine energy.

This heightened awareness allows you to:

- Trust your intuition more deeply
- Feel more connected to others and nature
- Embrace the cyclical rhythms of life
- Express yourself more authentically
- Nurture yourself and others with greater ease

By healing your inner child and cultivating your spiritual side, you're not just growing personally - you're tapping into the wellspring of feminine energy. This energy allows you to move through life with grace, empathy, and a profound sense of interconnectedness. You'll find yourself naturally embodying the nurturing, intuitive, and creative aspects of the divine feminine.

To deepen your spiritual connection and enhance your feminine energy, consider these practices:

1. Establish a Sacred Routine:
   - Create a daily spiritual practice
   - Quiet your mind through meditation or mindfulness
   - Open yourself to spiritual inspiration and guidance
2. Cultivate Deep Listening:
   - Attune to your heartbeat and inner rhythms
   - Practice mindful awareness of your surroundings
   - Trust your intuition and inner wisdom
3. Embrace Spirit Energy:
   - Allow energy to flow freely through you
   - Develop awareness of your inner voice
   - Trust in divine timing and synchronicity

To nurture your inner child and boost your feminine energy, try these exercises:
1. Playful Engagement:
   - Rediscover activities that bring you joy (e.g., hiking, dancing, painting)
   - Fully immerse yourself in the sensory experience
   - Allow yourself to be spontaneous and carefree
2. Self-Nurturing:
   - Comfort your inner child when feeling scared or sad
   - Practice self-compassion and gentle self-talk
   - Create a safe, nurturing environment for yourself
3. Spiritual Connection:
   - Engage in prayer or meditation
   - Cultivate trust in a higher power or universal energy
   - Release fears and negative emotions through spiritual practices
4. Emotional Expression:
   - Journal about your feelings and experiences
   - Express emotions through art, music, or movement
   - Share your feelings with trusted friends or a therapist
5. Sensory Exploration:
   - Engage in activities that stimulate your senses
   - Practice mindful eating, savoring each bite
   - Enjoy nature walks, focusing on the sights, sounds, and smells
6. Intuitive Development:
   - Practice following your gut feelings
   - Engage in activities like automatic writing or tarot reading
   - Trust your dreams and inner visions

By incorporating these practices, you'll deepen your spiritual connection while nurturing your inner child. This process naturally enhances your feminine energy, leading to greater emotional freedom, intuitive power, and a sense of connection to yourself and the world around you. Remember, this journey is unique to each individual - allow yourself to explore and discover what resonates most deeply with you.

YOUR SUPER POWER IS ALREADY IN YOU!

05

FEMININITY IS YOUR SUPERPOWER! PUT ON YOUR CAPE AND BE THE GODLY WOMAN YOU WERE BORN TO BE! BEAUTIFULLY ENCAPSULATES THE IDEA OF EMBRACING FEMININITY AS A SOURCE OF STRENGTH AND DIVINE PURPOSE.

LET'S EXPLORE SOME REAL-WORLD EXAMPLES OF WHAT THIS MIGHT LOOK LIKE:

1. Leadership with Compassion:
   - A female CEO who leads her company with both vision and empathy, fostering a nurturing work environment while achieving business goals.
   - A community leader who organizes support networks for local families, using her intuition and nurturing skills to identify and meet needs.

2. Creative Problem-Solving:
   - An environmental scientist who uses her connection with nature to develop innovative, eco-friendly solutions to climate challenges.
   - A mediator who leverages her emotional intelligence to resolve conflicts in a way that honors all parties involved.

3. Nurturing Health and Wellness:
   - A holistic health practitioner who combines modern medicine with intuitive healing practices to treat patients as whole beings.
   - A nutritionist who educates communities about nourishing their bodies, emphasizing the connection between food, emotions, and spiritual well-being.

> *Femininity is your superpower! Put on your cape and be the Godly woman you were born to be!*

4. Empowering Education:
   - A teacher who creates a classroom environment that nurtures creativity, emotional intelligence, and spiritual growth alongside academic learning.
   - A life coach who helps women reconnect with their inner wisdom and feminine power to achieve their goals.

5. Conscious Parenting:
   - A mother who raises her children with an emphasis on emotional intelligence, spiritual connection, and respect for all living beings.
   - A childcare provider who creates a nurturing environment that honors each child's unique spirit and potential.

6. Artistic Expression:
   - A visual artist whose work celebrates the divine feminine and inspires viewers to connect with their own inner goddess.
   - A musician whose lyrics and melodies touch hearts and heal souls, tapping into the universal language of emotion.

7. Spiritual Leadership:
   - A female religious leader who brings a nurturing, inclusive approach to her congregation, emphasizing love, compassion, and inner wisdom.
   - A yoga instructor who guides students to connect with their bodies, minds, and spirits, embodying the flow and grace of feminine energy.

8. Sustainable Business:
   - An entrepreneur who builds a company based on principles of nurturing the earth, fostering community, and promoting holistic well-being.
   - A fashion designer who creates clothing that honors and celebrates the female form in all its diverse beauty.

9. Healing and Counseling:
   - A therapist who incorporates feminine wisdom traditions into her practice, helping clients heal through connection with their inner selves and the natural world.

- A doula who supports women through pregnancy and childbirth, honoring the profound feminine power of creation.

10. Political Engagement:
- A politician who brings qualities of compassion, inclusivity, and long-term nurturing of community into her policy-making decisions.
- An activist who fights for social justice using methods of non-violent communication, emphasizing connection and understanding.

In each of these examples, women are using their feminine qualities - such as intuition, empathy, nurturing, creativity, and spiritual connection - as superpowers to make a positive impact in the world. We are embracing our roles as Godly women by embodying divine feminine qualities and using them to uplift, heal, and transform our spheres of influence.

LEARNING TO TRUST

06

As your inner child heals and you embrace your feminine energy, you may find yourself ready to open up to trust again. Trust is a cornerstone of feminine energy - it's about receptivity, openness, and connection.

Here's how to cultivate trust from this new, empowered feminine perspective:

Self-Trust First:
- Begin by trusting your own intuition and inner wisdom
- Honor your feelings and needs without judgment
- Practice self-compassion when you make mistakes

Gradual Openness:
- Start with small acts of trust in safe relationships
- Allow vulnerability in measured steps
- Celebrate each positive experience of trust

Embrace Imperfection:
- Recognize that everyone, including yourself, is fallible
- View mistakes as opportunities for growth and deeper understanding
- Release the need for perfectionism in yourself and others

Cultivate Discernment:
- Use your heightened intuition to gauge others' trustworthiness
- Pay attention to actions more than words
- Trust your gut feelings about situations and people

Practice Forgiveness:
- Forgive yourself for past trust issues
- Work on forgiving others who have broken your trust
- See forgiveness as a gift to yourself, not a pardon for others

Create a Nurturing Environment:
- Surround yourself with people who respect and honor trust
- Communicate your needs and boundaries clearly

- Foster relationships based on mutual respect and understanding

Embrace Vulnerability:
- Recognize that vulnerability is a strength, not a weakness
- Share your authentic self with trusted others
- Allow yourself to receive support and care

Trust the Lord:
- Cultivate faith in our Lord God
- Practice surrender and letting go of control
- Trust in the timing and unfolding of your life's journey

Remember, trust is a journey, not a destination. It's normal to have setbacks or moments of doubt. The key is to keep your heart open while maintaining healthy boundaries. As you continue to nurture your healed inner child and embrace your feminine energy, you'll find that trust becomes easier and more natural.

By approaching trust from this balanced, feminine perspective, you're not naive or overly guarded. Instead, you're discerning, open-hearted, and resilient. You're willing to risk being hurt because you know you have the strength to heal and grow from any experience.

Trust, like feminine energy, is fluid and adaptive. It ebbs and flows, strengthens and recalibrates. By embracing this fluidity, you allow yourself to experience the full richness of connections and relationships, enhancing your life and deepening your feminine power

LEARNING TO FORGIVE YOURSELF AND OTHERS

07

FORGIVENESS

*F*orgiveness is a powerful act of feminine energy, embodying compassion, emotional intelligence, and spiritual growth. As a woman leading with feminine energy, here's how to approach forgiveness

Distinguish Between Forgetting and Forgiving: Feminine energy acknowledges the full spectrum of emotions. Forgiveness doesn't mean erasing memories, but transforming their emotional charge. Allow yourself to feel, process, and then release, using your intuitive wisdom to guide this journey.

Embrace Reality with Compassion: Feminine energy is grounded in truth and nurturing. Accept what has happened by approaching it with curiosity and compassion. Listen to others' perspectives with an open heart, fostering understanding and connection

Seek Forgiveness with Authenticity: When asking for forgiveness, tap into your feminine vulnerability. Communicate with honesty and emotional depth. This genuine approach, rooted in self-awareness, can create powerful healing connections.

Practice Self-Forgiveness as Self-Love: Self-forgiveness is a profound act of self-nurturing, a cornerstone of feminine energy. Treat yourself with the same compassion you'd offer a dear friend. This self-love radiates outward, positively impacting all your relationships.

> *"Forgiveness is a powerful act of feminine energy, embodying compassion, emotional intelligence, and spiritual growth."*

Celebrate Imperfection as Growth: Feminine energy embraces the cyclical nature of life, including growth through mistakes. View imperfections as opportunities for evolution. This perspective fosters resilience and a deeper connection with your authentic self.

Seek Support and Guidance: Embracing support is a strength of feminine energy. Whether through therapy, mentorship, or spiritual guidance, allow yourself to be held and guided. This receptivity to support can deepen your forgiveness journey.

Cultivate Empathy Through Perspective-Taking:
Use your feminine gift of empathy to understand others' actions. This doesn't justify harmful behavior but can provide context and ease the path to forgiveness.

Practice Forgiveness as a Ongoing Process: Forgiveness, like feminine energy, is fluid and cyclical. It's not a one-time event but an ongoing practice. Allow yourself to revisit and refine your forgiveness as you grow and evolve.

Practice Forgiveness as a Ongoing Process:

Forgiveness, like feminine energy, is fluid and cyclical. It's not a one-time event but an ongoing practice. Allow yourself to revisit and refine your forgiveness as you grow and evolve.

As a woman embracing her feminine energy, forgiveness becomes a superpower. It allows you to maintain your open heart while setting healthy boundaries. It enables you to transform pain into wisdom, resentment into compassion, and fear into love.

Through forgiveness, you tap into the divine feminine qualities of creation, transformation, and renewal. You become a force of healing, not just for yourself, but for your relationships and community. This forgiveness-centered approach to life enhances your intuition, deepens your connections, and amplifies your feminine radiance.

Remember, forgiveness doesn't mean tolerating abuse or remaining in harmful situations. It's about freeing yourself emotionally and spiritually, allowing you to make clear, empowered decisions from a place of inner peace rather than reactivity.

By embracing forgiveness as an integral part of your feminine journey, you're not just healing past wounds – you're actively creating a more compassionate, understanding, and harmonious world. This is the true power of a woman leading with her divine feminine energy

TOOLS TO TAP INTO YOUR GODLY FEMININITY

08

THE TOOLS

Daily Ritual Practice

Sisterhood Circles

Intuition Journaling

Gratitude for Your Feminine Body

Sacred Sexuality Practice

Creativity Dates

Daily Ritual Practice:

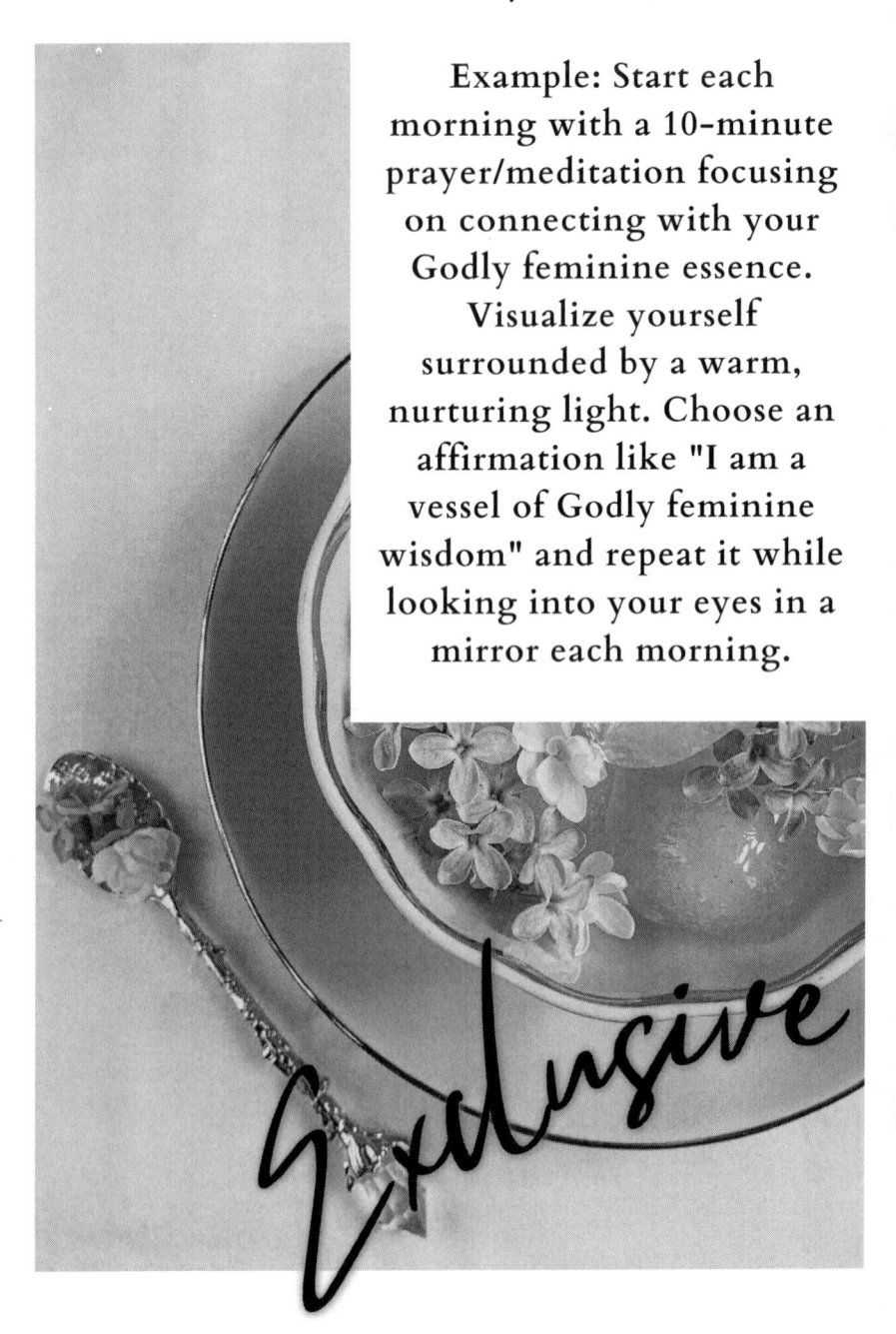

Example: Start each morning with a 10-minute prayer/meditation focusing on connecting with your Godly feminine essence. Visualize yourself surrounded by a warm, nurturing light. Choose an affirmation like "I am a vessel of Godly feminine wisdom" and repeat it while looking into your eyes in a mirror each morning.

Creativity Dates:

Example: Schedule a weekly "date" with your creative self. Use this time to write, paint, sing, or express yourself creatively without judgment. Get dressed and have dinner at a 5-star restaurant with yourself!

Sacred Sexuality Practice:

Example: Explore tantric breathing exercises with a partner or solo, focusing on the divine energy flowing through your body. Treat yourself to some beautiful lingerie. Sleeping in gowns and pajamas versus a t-shirt and shorts goes a long way.

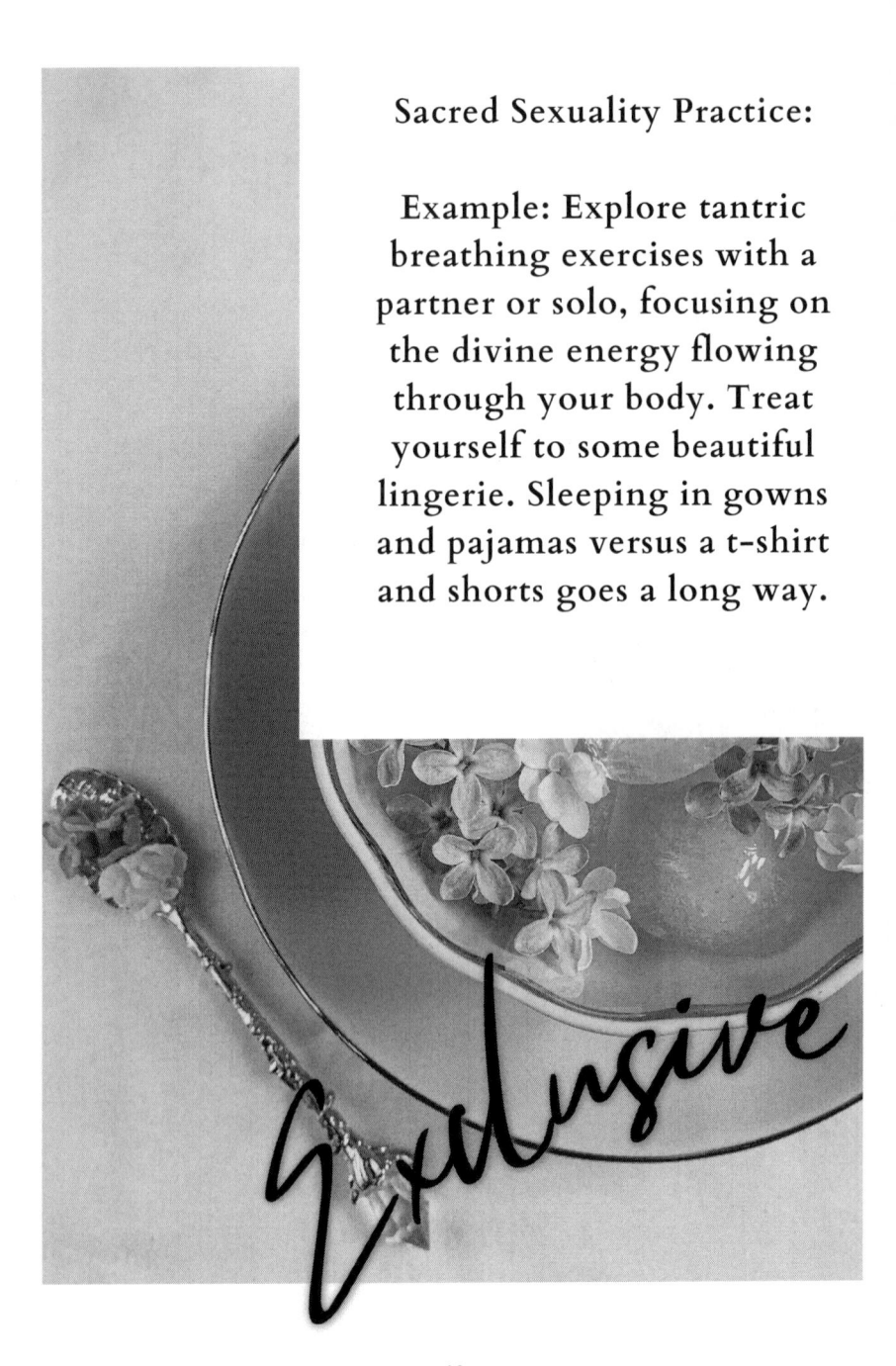

Sisterhood Circles:

Example: Organize a monthly women's circle where you can share, support each other, and practice feminine rituals together.

Seek out a woman you admire for her embodiment of feminine energy and ask her to mentor you. Alternatively, become a mentor to a younger woman.

Intuition Journaling:

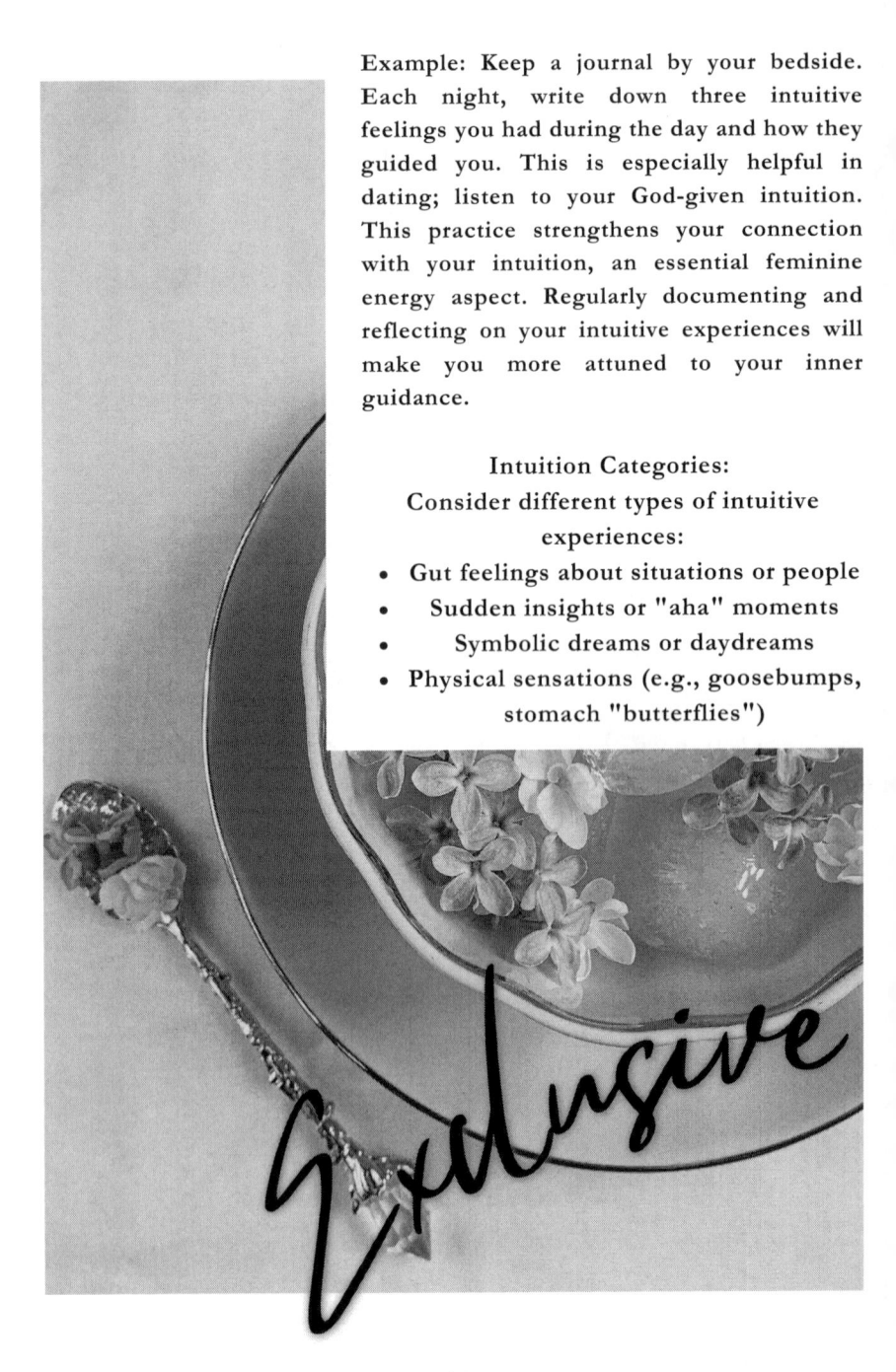

Example: Keep a journal by your bedside. Each night, write down three intuitive feelings you had during the day and how they guided you. This is especially helpful in dating; listen to your God-given intuition. This practice strengthens your connection with your intuition, an essential feminine energy aspect. Regularly documenting and reflecting on your intuitive experiences will make you more attuned to your inner guidance.

Intuition Categories:
Consider different types of intuitive experiences:
- Gut feelings about situations or people
- Sudden insights or "aha" moments
- Symbolic dreams or daydreams
- Physical sensations (e.g., goosebumps, stomach "butterflies")

Gratitude for Your Feminine Body: Embracing and Honoring Your Divine Form

This practice is about cultivating a deep appreciation for your body as a sacred vessel of feminine energy. It's a powerful way to counteract societal messages that often lead women to criticize or feel dissatisfied with their bodies. Each morning or evening, stand in front of a mirror. Focus on a different part of your body. Express genuine gratitude for its function, beauty, and feminine qualities

Example Practice: "Today, I thank my hands. I appreciate their strength and gentleness. I'm grateful for how they allow me to create, to comfort, to connect. These hands have the power to nurture, to heal, to express love. They are beautiful in their uniqueness, carrying the wisdom of all the women in my lineage. Thank you, hands, for being a channel of my feminine energy in the world. How can I honor and nurture you today?"

By consistently practicing this kind of deep, specific gratitude for your feminine body, you cultivate a profound sense of self-love and connection to your divine feminine nature. This practice helps shift your relationship with your body from criticism to reverence, allowing you to more fully embody and express your feminine energy in all aspects of your life.

Receptivity Training:

Example: Practice saying "yes" to offers of help for a week, allowing yourself to receive support and nurturing from others. This practice is designed to cultivate the feminine quality of receptivity, which is often challenging for women who are used to giving or doing everything themselves.

Mindful Acceptance:
When someone offers help, pause and take a deep breath before responding. Notice any discomfort or resistance that arises. Consciously choose to accept the offer, even if it feels uncomfortable.

Gratitude Expression:
When you receive help or a gift, express genuine gratitude.

Compliment Acceptance:
When given a compliment, resist the urge to deflect or minimize it.
Instead, simply say "Thank you" and allow yourself to truly receive the positive words.

Energetic Boundaries:
While practicing receptivity, also tune into your boundaries. Learn to discern between genuine offers and those that don't feel right to accept.

Remember, receptivity is a strength, not a weakness. It allows for a balanced exchange of energy and creates space for more abundance and support in your life. By practicing receptivity, you're embodying an essential aspect of feminine energy and creating a more harmonious, interconnected way of living.

Remember, the key is consistency and authenticity. Choose the tools that resonate most with you and make them a regular part of your life. As you practice, you'll find yourself naturally embodying more of your divine feminine energy in all aspects of your life.

THE WORKBOOK

09

This workbook structure allows for daily engagement with different aspects of feminine energy, encouraging regular practice and reflection. It provides a balanced approach to nurturing, expressing, and living in alignment with one's feminine power.

As you embrace your new journey, each page could include:

- An inspiring quote about feminine energy or empowerment
- A small ritual or practice suggestion related to the page's theme
- A scale to rate your connection to your feminine energy that day
- A prompt for deeper reflection

Connecting with Your Divine Feminine

- Section for daily feminine energy check-in

_____
_____
_____
_____

- Space to note intuitive feelings and insights

_____
_____
_____
_____

- Area to record daily gratitude for feminine qualities

_____
_____
_____
_____

- Prompt for a daily feminine energy affirmation

_____
_____
_____
_____

Nurturing Your Feminine Body

- Body mapping exercise: outline of a female body to shade areas of gratitude/tension

_____
_____
_____
_____

- Daily body appreciation entry

_____
_____
_____
_____

- Section to note how you nurtured your body today

_____
_____
_____
_____

- Space to record any physical sensations or intuitions

_____
_____
_____
_____

Cultivating Receptivity and Trust

- "Receiving Log": space to record instances of allowing yourself to receive

_____

_____

_____

_____

- Section to note any resistance to receiving and reflections on why

_____

_____

_____

_____

- Trust-building exercise: noting one way you trusted your intuition today

_____

_____

_____

_____

- Area to plan one way to practice receptivity tomorrow

_____

_____

_____

_____

Expressing Your Feminine Power

- Creative expression section: space for doodles, poetry, or free writing

_____

_____

_____

_____

- "Feminine Wisdom in Action": noting how you applied feminine principles in daily life

_____

_____

_____

_____

- Reflection on balancing feminine and masculine energies

_____

_____

_____

_____

- Weekly review: celebrating growth and setting intentions for further embracing feminine energy

_____

_____

_____

_____

THANK YOU SO MUCH!

To my amazing parents, Rev. Dr. Paul E. and Pamela H. Hemphill, I love you two so much. Thank you for instilling in me much of the content in this book. Your Godly wisdom and encouragement are my foundation! Mommie, you are the epitome of femininity, and Dad, thank you for showing me what a man, leader, and Godly masculine man looks like! To my beautiful sisters Starr and Phylicia Rose, I love you and really appreciate your support!

The following individuals believed in my vision and purpose! Thank you for being the first to purchase! :

Amanda Brown Simpson
Angela Gravely Harris
Anthony McCarver
Arnita Dula
Cleveland Huntley
Darlene Lease
Deborah Ally
Deirdre Pippins
Dr. Pearl Burris-Floyd
Harold K Sublett
Icey Dyanne
Ingrid Hence
Jody Yearwood
Kim Lindstrom
Kimberly Parker
Lee
Lilo
Lisa Hailey
Lisa Sido
Makeisha Griffin

Maurice Ball
Maurice Coney
Miriam Gomillion
Misha Bucholtz
MzNikkiD
Natalie Lowe
Pandora Prater
Reeshemah Norris
Regina Taylor
Renee Davis
Robin Hall
Sandra Harris
Shawnya Gore
SydneyKelliee
Sylvia Thomas
Tenia Friday-Taylor
Theresa Prince
Toni Godfrey
Valerie Waddell
Vivian McLean Taylor

WHAT OTHERS HAVE TO SAY

"Angel's profound expertise, extensive experience, and deep understanding of femininity have empowered countless women, including myself, to embrace our superpowers with grace and strength. She fosters a supportive environment where women confidently assert their power in both personal and professional relationships. Angel compassionately addresses the needs of women navigating healing from childhood experiences that have impacted their confidence"

Delanda Charleston, PHR
Team Charleston Travel, Owner

"I have had the privilege of being personally coached by Angel in both a private setting and via her many live appearances. I have learned a great deal when it comes to femininity from her. In our group chats, there have been many occasions where individuals have typical female responses to situations. Angel always brings a different perspective and can present them in a way that provides much introspection and allows us to consider alternatives that may produce a better outcome. Her chats promote deeper thought processes and allow me to think about situations from a broader perspective. I've learned different techniques on how to utilize my femininity to get the outcome I desire while at the same time giving my partner what he needs as well."

Atalaya Benn, Graphic Designer
Affectionately Designed

When I met Angel in 2022, I never thought we would end up here(Besties). I also had no idea of all of the knowledge and information she possessed. She caused me to realize things about myself that I never really considered before when it comes to my own personal femininity. Angel has become my go-to person for all things feminine. I love the fact that we have developed a relationship where she is just one call away. To watch her approach to situations is unreal. Nothing but poise and grace flows out of her. I am so proud to be able to call her a friend.

Tonya Jenkins, Certified Life Coach, and Author
SHE Matters Academy, LLC

"Angel Carmell is sure to shake you up as she takes you on a transformative journey that every woman should embark upon. With profound wisdom and compassionate guidance, Angel delves into the essence of feminine strength, offering powerful insights and practical tools for healing the wounds of the past. She has a unique flair and care for her clients and in this book Her empathetic and empowering approach not only nurtures the inner child but also awakens a deeper sense of self-love and resilience. This book is a must-read for anyone seeking to embrace their true feminine power and live a life of authenticity and joy. Highly recommended for women of all ages who are ready to heal, grow, and thrive."

Sydney Kelliee, Author and
Women's Certified Life Coach

Made in the USA
Columbia, SC
22 September 2024